CONTENTS

Copyright ©2020 ARNOLD KUNTZ PH.D

INTRODUCTION

You don't have to own a large estate to grow a wide variety of fruits at home. If you don't have space for full-sized trees, you can plant dwarf forms of apples, pears and other fruits. Or try pruning and training trees on a trellis in the time-honored technique known as espalier. Grow a grapevine over an arbor or pergola. Plant lowbush blueberries or strawberries in a bed near the house. Even container growing is possible, giving northern gardeners a chance to grow citrus, figs and other frost-tender fruit trees.

When you grow your own fruits and vegetables, you get all the fun of gardening plus the garden-to-table goodness and nutrition that only comes with homegrown harvests.

Most people love fruit but not everyone is confident enough for growing fruits in the garden. Don't let this deter you. Whether a seasoned gardener or just starting out, creating an edible fruit garden is easy. From common types of fruit (strawberries, watermelons, etc.) to tropical fruit tree growing (lemons, kumquats, etc.), there's something here for everyone. Use these tips on growing fruits in the garden and you'll be on your way to eating home-grown fruit of your very own.

CHAPTER ONE

Gardening, the laying out and care of a plot of ground devoted partially or wholly to the growing of plants such as flowers, herbs, or vegetables.

Gardening can be considered both as an art, concerned with arranging plants harmoniously in their surroundings, and as a science, encompassing the principles and techniques of plant cultivation. Because plants are often grown in conditions markedly different from those of their natural environment, it is necessary to apply to their cultivation techniques derived from plant physiology, chemistry, and botany, modified by the experience of the planter. The basic principles involved in growing plants are the same in all parts of the world, but the practice naturally needs much adaptation to local conditions.

For the main history of garden development, see the article garden and landscape design: Historical development.

THE NATURE OF GARDENING

Gardening in its ornamental sense needs a certain level of civilization before it can flourish. Wherever that level has been attained, in all parts of the world and at all periods, people have made efforts to shape their environment into an attractive display. The instinct and even enthusiasm for gardening thus appear to arise from some primitive response to nature, engendering a wish to produce growth and harmony in a creative partnership with it.

It is possible to be merely an admiring spectator of gardens. However, most people who cultivate a domestic plot also derive satisfaction from involvement in the processes of tending plants. They find that the necessary attention to the seasonal changes, and to the myriad small "events" in any shrubbery or herbaceous border, improves their understanding and appreciation of gardens in general.

A phenomenal upsurge of interest in gardening began in Western countries after World War II. A lawn with flower beds and perhaps a vegetable patch has become a sought-after advantage to home ownership. The increased interest produced an unprecedented expansion of business among horticultural suppliers, nurseries, garden centres, and seedsmen. Books, journals, and newspaper

columns on garden practice have found an eager reader-
ship, while television and radio programs on the subject
have achieved a dedicated following.

Several reasons for this expansion suggest themselves. Increased leisurein the industrial nations gives more people
the opportunity to enjoy this relaxing pursuit. The increased public appetite for self-sufficiency in basic skills
also encourages people to take up the spade. In the
kitchen, the homegrown potato or ear of sweet corn
rewards the gardener with a sense of achievement, as
well as with flavour superior to that of store-bought produce. An increased awareness of threats to the natural
environment and the drabness of many inner cities stir
some people to cultivate the greenery and colour around
their own doorsteps. The bustle of 20th-century life leads
more individuals to rediscover the age-old tranquillity of
gardens.

CHOICE OF PLANTS

The need for cooperation with nature is probably most felt by the amateur gardener in choosing the plants he wants to grow. The range of plants available to the modern gardener is remarkably rich, and new varieties are constantly being offered by nurseries. Most of the shrubs and flowers used in the Western world are descendants of plants imported from other countries. Because they are nonnative, they present the gardener with some of his most interesting problems but also with the possibility of an enhanced display. Plants that originated in subtropical regions, for example, are naturally more sensitive to frost. Some, like rhododendrons or azaleas, originated in an acid soil, mainly composed of leaf mold. Consequently, they will not thrive in a chalky or an alkaline soil. Plant breeding continues to improve the adaptability of such exotic plants, but the more closely the new habitat resembles the original, the better the plant will flourish. Manuals offer solutions to most such problems, and the true gardener will always enjoy finding his own. In such experiments, he may best experience his work as part of the historical tradition of gardening.

HISTORICAL BACKGROUND

Early history

Western gardening had its origins in Egypt some 4,000 years ago. As the style spread, it was changed and adapted to different localities and climates, but its essentials remained those of disciplined lines and groupings of plants, usually in walled enclosures. Gardening was introduced into Europe through the expansion of Roman rule and, second, by way of the spread of Islam into Spain. Though clear evidence is lacking, it is presumed that Roman villas outside the confines of Italy contained native and imported plants, hedges, fruit trees, and vines, in addition to herbs for medicinal and culinary purposes.

In medieval times the monasteries were the main repositories of gardening knowledge and the important herbal lore. Though little is certainly known about the design and content of the monastic garden, it probably consisted of a walled courtyard built around a well or an arbour, with colour provided by flowers (some of which, including roses and lilies, served as ecclesiastical symbols), all of which maintained the ancient idea of the garden as a place of contemplation.

The earliest account of gardening in English, The Feate of Gardening, dating from about 1400, mentions the use of more than 100 plants, with instructions on sowing, planting, and grafting of trees and advice on cultivation of herbs such as parsley, sage, fennel, thyme, camomile, and saffron. The vegetables mentioned include turnip, spinach, leek, lettuce, and garlic.

Early gardening was largely for utility. The emergence of the garden as a form of creative display properly began in the 16th century. The Renaissance, with its increased prosperity, brought an upsurge of curiosity about the natural world and, incidentally, stirred interest in composing harmonious forms in the garden.

This awakening took especially firm root in Elizabethan England, which notably developed the idea that gardens were for enjoyment and delight. Echoing the Renaissance outlook, the mood of the period was one of exuberance in gardening, seen in the somewhat playful arrangements of Tudor times, with mazes, painted statuary, and knot gardens (consisting of beds in which various types of plants were separated by dwarf hedges). Flowers began to appear profusely in paintings and, as mentioned above, were used by poets in their verbal images.

This enthusiasm was accompanied by an earnest search for knowledge, and the period saw the birth of botanical science. A leading figure in this work was Carolus Clusius (Charles de l'Écluse), whose botanical skills and introduction of the tulip and other bulbous plants to the botanical gardens at Leiden, Netherlands, laid the foundation for Dutch prominence in international horticulture. The earliest botanical gardenwas that of Pisa (1543), followed by that of Padua (1545). The first in England was founded at Oxford in 1621, followed by

Scotland's first, at Edinburgh, in 1667. The gardens at Kew, near London, were founded almost a century later, in 1759. These centres of experiment and learning have contributed greatly to the art and science of horticulture.

The advances from the simple medieval style were marked and rapid at this time. The English statesman and scholar Francis Bacon could already, by 1625, advance a sophisticated and almost modern conceptionof the garden in his essay "On Gardens." He saw it as a place that should be planted for year-round enjoyment, offering a wide range of experiences through colour, form and scent, exercise and repose. The flower garden, already well established by the early 17th century, was set against a background of tall, clipped hedges and neatly scythed lawns. The taste of the time, as contemporary lists show, was for perfumed varieties such as carnations, lavender, sweet marjoram, musk roses, and poppies.

The plant trade
As interest in gardening developed in Europe, the new trade of nurseryman was established, and the trade became highly important to the spread of knowledge and materials. By the end of the 17th century, nurserymen were relatively numerous in England, France, and the Low Countries, with keen customers among the nobility and gentry for all the exotica they could provide. The catalog of the Tradescant family's private botanical garden in London listed 1,600 plants in 1656. A number of them had been brought back by the family from visits to Virginia. These early exotica from the New World included now familiar plants such as the Michaelmas daisy, the Virginia creeper, hamamelis, goldenrod, the first perennial lupine, and such fine autumn-colouring trees as liquidambar and

the staghorn sumac. The work of the nurserymen thus spread new plants more widely and, as breeding skills developed, contributed to the acclimatizing of foreign imports.

Vegetables and fruits

The history of vegetables is imprecise. Though familiar types, including the radish, turnip, and onion, are known to have been in cultivation from early times, it is fairly supposed that they were meagre and would bear little clear resemblance to modern equivalents. The early range available to European gardens and, later, to those in America, included such native plants as kale, parsnips, and the Brussels sprout family, with peas and broad beans grown as field crops.

The Romans introduced the globe artichoke, leek, cucumber, cabbage, asparagus, and the Mediterranean strain of garlic to their imperial territory wherever these plants would flourish. Among plants imported to Europe from the Americas were the scarlet runner bean and tomato (both originally grown for ornament), corn (maize), and the vastly important potato. The numerous herbs in use were mostly native to European locations. One curiosity to the modern mind is that certain flowers, such as marigolds, violets, and primroses, were used as flavourings in the kitchen.

The cultivation of fruit trees was one of the most advanced skills and interests from the 16th century onward. Pride was taken in variety, and, judging by the opulent still-life paintings of the period, the quality was remarkably high. Among the challenges bravely taken up in the 17th century in northern Europe was the growing of orange and lemon trees, though this was done more for the pleasure of their evergreen qualities than for their fruit. The catalog of the British royal gardens in 1708 shows 14 varieties of cherry, 14 apricots, 58 kinds of peach and nectarine, 33 plums, eight figs, 23 vines, 29 pears, and numerous varieties of apple.

The plant hunters

The early importation of plants to Europe was managed through informal channels, following the increase in exploration and the spread of empires. Seeds and tubers were sent home by diplomats and missionaries, sea captains and travelers. An example of this type of collecting is afforded by Henry Compton, bishop of London, whose diocese included the American colonies. He was an avid collector, and he corresponded with likeminded experts in Europe and America and thus brought numerous fine plants to his exceptional garden in Fulham, west London. He also encouraged his missionaries to send home seeds. From one such source in Virginia came the Magnolia virginiana, the first magnolia to be cultivated. This was the beginning of what became known as the American garden, based upon magnolias, azaleas, and other woodland species.

As the appetite for exotica developed, plant collecting around the world became more systematized. Expeditions to foreign parts were organized and financed by nurserymen, botanical gardens, or syndicates of private gardeners. The botanist plant hunters thus sent out were exceptional and patient. They were required to endure long voyages and residence for up to several years in an often hostile environment. Their goal was to find the plant in flower, return in due season to collect seed, then see their delicate specimens back to Europe through varying climatic zones.

North America's potential to yield countless new specimens was recognized early: the first book on American plants, published in London in 1577, was entitled Joyfull Newes out of the New Founde Worlde and was in itself a hint of the excited spirit of contemporary gardening. The jacaranda, flowering catalpa, and wisteria were among the finds made by Compton's missionaries in the Carolinas. An early resident collector in North America was John Bartram, regarded as the founder of American botany. He settled on a farm near Philadelphia in 1728 and, in 30 years of collecting in the Alleghenies, Carolinas, and other areas of North America, sent some 200 important plants to British gardens in sufficient quantity that they became widespread there.

The extremely rich west coast of North America was not exploited by plant collectors until the early 19th century. The contemporary importance of such discoveries is suggested by the fact that, in their celebrated crossing of the American continent in 1804–06, Lewis and Clark found time to collect the seeds of Mahonia aquifolium and Symphoricarpos racemosus. Perhaps the most distinguished collector among an exceptional fraternity was David Douglas, one of the numerous Scotsmen who contributed to international botany. His expeditions to the North American Far West brought to Europe such important timber trees as the Douglas fir, the Sitka spruce, the Monterey pine, and a number of now familiar shrubs such as Garrya elliptica and Ribes sanguineum. The California annuals he discovered made a lasting impact on the colour of Western gardens. In the 19th century, plant collectors began to explore South America, where two Cornish brothers, William and Thomas Lobb, gained prominence. They are credited with carrying back to Europe the monkey puzzle tree (Araucaria araucana), native to the Andes mountains; the Berberis darwinii; and the Escallonia macrantha.

Branch of the monkey puzzle tree (Araucaria araucana), an evergreen ornamental and timber conifer native to the Andes mountains of South America.

Collectors went to a number of countries in the 19th century, but the most important area was China. Its flora was more intact than that in the West, because the erosions of the Ice Age had been less severe for climatic reasons, and it had a long history of skilled gardening. Plant collection was difficult, however, because for many years the only foreigners allowed to travel within its borders were Jesuit priests. They aided botanists by sending many specimens to Paris and London. The first professional collector to live in China was William Kerr, who sent out 238 new plants. Real exploration of the interior did not begin until the 1840s. China, Japan, and the Himalayas produced unparalleled riches in rhododendrons, azaleas, flowering cherries, ornamental maples, roses, lilies, primulas, poppies, kerrias, and quinces.

The conditions for transporting plants from such distances had been much improved by Nathaniel B. Ward's invention of the wardian case, an airtight glass box that protected the plants from sea air and harsh climate. Gradually almost all regions and countries were visited, and new plants and their progeny were dispersed around the Western world. And still the search for new specimens continues.

From the 19th century

By the early 19th century, with the expansion of the horticultural trade, gardening had become international in scope. Numerous handbooks spread knowledge. The founding of new garden and botanical societies, such as the London (later Royal) Horticultural Society, helped to increase interest, encourage science, and raise standards. Such moves signaled the rise of the small leisure gardener; a floral retreat was no longer the sole property of the rich. It now extended from the manor to the small suburban garden.

Gardens in North America had generally been smaller and trimmer than their European counterparts, with box edgings and pleached trees (that is, lines of trees allowed to grow with branches interlaced to form a screen), as seen in the reconstructed gardens of Williamsburg, Virginia. The "natural" gardening style (known on the European continent as the English style), which had overtaken earlier formality, allowed wider use of plant varieties. This approach became the pervasive trend in the west, notably through the views of John Claudius Loudon, whose Encyclopaedia of Gardening (1822) set the pattern of domestic cultivation over a long period with a style known as Gardenesque. His style encouraged the individual qualities of garden elements while ensuring that together they made a harmonious blend.

The natural style was further enhanced by an English artist and landscape architect, Gertrude Jekyll. In her opinion, the first purpose of a garden is to give happiness and repose of mind. With experience derived from the richly floral cottage gardens of Surrey, she developed the idea of supporting plants with an architectural base and allowing them to grow in a free form, encouraging natural shape and creating harmonious relationships of colour.

The period saw much progress in garden equipment and supplies. Heated greenhouses had been in use since the late 17th century, and mass production led to great strides in nursery gardening. The modern, bladed lawn mower was first seen in a design of 1832; in more recent times the application of the jet-engine principle led to the hover mower. Fertilizer development was also important, from the discovery of superphosphate to the devising of modern kinds of foliar feeding.

In the second half of the 20th century, interest in gardening brought in new adherents in unprecedented numbers; they were advised and encouraged by numerous publications and by television and radio programs. Though the process was very gradual, domestic gardening became somewhat more adventurous. Among the more ambitious, designs took a multiplicity of forms, from the Japanese garden, producing an austere magic out of rock and pebble, to the other extreme of the wild country garden, virtually left to seed itself. Increasing numbers of professional designers at their best set high standards to emulate. But the art of gardening still depends on a simple empathy with the needs and nature of living things. Symbolic of this essential, the spade has remained much the same implement that it had been in medieval times.

HOW TO START A NEW GARDEN

You may have visions of drifts of color, wildflower prairies, or bushels of tomatoes, but get your feet wet first with some gardening basics. For flower gardens, choose a site close to the door or with a good view from a favorite window. Place your garden where you'll see and enjoy it often. This will also motivate you to garden more.

The front lawn shown here is small, but the homeowners still found an attractive, sunny spot to add some color and curb appeal. No matter how busy they are, they can enjoy their garden every time they pull into their driveway or look out their front window.

Evaluate and Choose a Site

If you have your heart set on growing a specific plant, check to see what growing conditions it requires. Vegetables will need at least six hours of sun exposure a day. The same goes for most flowering plants. However, there are still many to choose from for a partially shaded site. If you want to start a garden where there is mostly shade, your choices are going to be more limited but not prohibitive.

The folks in this picture have a partially shaded front entrance. They could easily add a small garden along the walkway where they could enjoy it, making their entrance more of a focal point.

Also, take into consideration when the sun hits your site. The afternoon sun will be hotter and more drying than the morning sun. Many plants turn their faces toward the sun, so if your view of the garden is from a west window, your flowers may face away from you in the afternoon. Evaluate other elements of exposure such as high, drying winds or heavy foot traffic.

Once you know where you'd like to try your first garden, you must use a hose or extension cord to try laying it out on the ground. Figure out the space it will take up.

Examine the Soil

Once you know where you want to plant, it's time to check the soil. Soil testing is the least glamorous part of gardening, but the most important. At the very least, check your soil's pH. This will tell you how acid or alkaline your soil is. Plants cannot take up nutrients unless the soil's pH is within an acceptable range. Most plants like a somewhat neutral pH, 6.2 to 6.8, but some are even more particular than that. If you are growing plants from the nursery, check the plant tag for specifics. If no pH preference is listed, a neutral range is fine.

You may also want to check the texture of your soil or even the nutrients and minerals in it. You can have that done at your local Cooperative Extension office and some nurseries. Soil texture refers to whether it is sandy, heavy clay, rocky, or the ideal sandy loam. Whatever the texture, it can be improved with the addition of organic matter such as compost.

Prepare the Bed

This is no one's favorite garden chore, but there's no way around it. Your chosen site will probably have grass on it or at least weeds. These must be cleared somehow before you can plant anything. Tilling without removing the grass or weeds is best done in the fall so that the grass will have a chance to begin decomposing during the winter. Even so, you will probably see new grass and weeds emerging in the spring. It's better to either remove the existing vegetation completely or to smother it.

A sharp flat-edged spade can be used to slice out the sod. If you have poor soil and need to amend it with organic matter or other nutrients, removing the sod may be your best bet so that you can till in the amendments.

Removing sod can be heavy work, and you wind up losing good topsoil along with the sod. If your soil is in relatively good shape, it is possible to leave the grass in place and build on top of it. Place a thick layer (eight to 10 sheets) of newspaper over the garden bed and wet it thoroughly. Then cover the newspaper with 4 to 6 inches of good soil. The newspaper will eventually decompose, and the turf and weeds will be smothered. There may be some defiant weeds that poke through, but not so many you can hand weed them.

Starting with good soil means you won't have to add a lot of artificial fertilizer to your garden. If you've fed the soil with amendments, the soil will feed your plants.

CHOOSING WHAT YOU'D LIKE TO GROW

This is harder than you might think. If you are starting small, you have to limit yourself to a handful of plants. If you are growing vegetables, you must start with what you like to eat and what you can't find fresh locally. Corn takes a lot of space and remains in the garden a long time before it's ready to be eaten. If you have corn farms nearby, you might want to use your small garden for vegetables that give a longer harvest such as tomatoes, lettuce, and beans.

Flower gardens can be even harder. Start with what colors you like. Rather than basing your dream on a photograph from a magazine, take a look at what your neighbors are growing successfully. They may even be able to give you a division or two.

Take a walk around a couple of garden centers and read the plant labels. Then play with combining the plants that strike your eye until you find a combination of three to five plants that please you. Make sure all the plants have the same growing requirements (sun, water, pH, etc.) and that none of them are going to require more care than you can give them.

Keep the variety of plants limited. It makes a better composition to have more plants of fewer varieties than to have one of this and one of that.

Planting

Sometimes you have to plant when you have the time, even if that's high noon on a Saturday. But the ideal time to plant is on a still, overcast day. The point is, stress your new plants as little as possible.

• Water the plants in their pots the day before you intend to plant.

• Don't remove all the plants from their pots and leave them sitting in the sun for the roots to dry out.

• If the roots are densely packed or growing in a circle, tease them apart so they will stretch out and grow into the surrounding soil.

• Bury the plant to the depth it was in the pot. Too deep and the stem will rot. Too high and the roots will dry out.

• Don't press down hard on the plants as you cover them. Watering will settle them into the ground.

• Water your newly planted garden as soon as it is planted and make sure it gets at least 1 inch of water per week. You may have to water more often in hot, dry summers. Let your plants tell you how much water they need. Some wilting in noonday sun is normal. Wilting in the evening is stress.

Mulch

You hear a lot about mulching lately, but it does make a major difference in a garden. Mulch conserves water, blocks weeds, and cools the soil. Organic mulches such as shredded or chipped bark, compost, straw, and shredded leaves will also improve the soil's quality.

Plastic mulches are nice in a vegetable garden to heat the soil around warm-season crops such as tomatoes, peppers, melons, and squash.

Whatever mulch you choose, apply it soon after planting, before new weeds sprout. Apply a 2- to 4-inch-thick layer of mulch, avoiding direct contact with the plant stems. Piling mulch around the stem can lead to rotting and can provide cover for munching mice and voles.

LABEL YOUR PLANTS AND KEEP GARDEN RECORDS

Keep a record of what you have planted or, better yet, keep the labels that came with your plants. This will help answer any questions about what the plant may need if it starts looking poorly and will remind you next year of what you liked and what didn't work. It also helps to take pictures and label them. You'll remember color combinations and favorite plants.

If you start a garden journal, you can also record how plants perform, when flowers are in bloom, how large the harvest was, and all kinds of information that will help you make a better garden next year.

WHAT TO EXPECT WITH GARDEN MAINTENANCE

Hopefully, when you were selecting plants, you did some background checking and didn't select too many prima donnas. All plants are going to require some maintenance. The idea that perennial plants require less maintenance than annuals is wrong.

• At the very least, your plants will require one inch of water a week. If it rains regularly, that is good for you. If it does not, don't let your plants get drought-stressed. Once a plant is stressed, it will not recover during that growing season.

• There will also be some weeding to do. Weed seeds come from all kinds of sources: wind, birds, soil on shoes, etc.

• Deadheading or removing the spent blossoms from your flowers will keep them blooming longer and looking fresher. Vegetables will produce more if you keep harvesting while young.

• Some taller plants may need to be staked to keep from flopping.

It may happen that one of your choices isn't happy and dies. Move on and replace it with something else.

COMMON GARDENING MISTAKES

Gardeners seem to prefer learning the hard way. In spite of all the gardening books we browse through, and the classes we attend, mistakes are invariably made.

Here's a sample of the ones many have made and regretted.

Not Preparing the Beds

- Most of us have made this mistake, some out of ignorance, and others due to sheer laziness.
- When the little seeds and seedling go into the damp earth in spring, it seems the tiny planting holes we make with our fingers or a small hand shovel are room enough for them.
- But the soil soon dries out and becomes rock hard. If the roots of the young plants cannot penetrate into the soil, you'll end up with stunted plants.
- Digging and double digging the garden beds and adding in plenty of compost and leaf mold

makes the soil loose enough for good root run. And this backbreaking work has to be done before you plant things.

- Making raised beds is another option if you don't want to dig deep.

Leaving out Soil Amendment

- We tend to forget that soil is like a living organism, always changing and evolving.
- Soil conditions can fluctuate with the amount of rainfall, soil runoff and lack of drainage. Some plants deplete certain soil nutrients more than the others.
- Heavy rains can leach away the limestone you recently added to raise the pH of your broccoli bed.
- It pays to check the soil for pH level and mineral profile every growing season and make necessary amendments a few weeks before planting time.
- Then test again to make sure things are perfect for the plants that are getting ready to go in.
- Organic matter has a modulating effect on soil chemistry, so the more humus your soil has, the lesser the chemical fluctuations.
- Add plenty of compost and cured manure to your vegetable beds.
- Good soil is particularly important for your veggies garden since you need healthy plants that produce high-quality food.

Overwatering

- Overwatering is like killing with too much

- love. Most over enthusiastic gardeners are guilty of this crime.
- Frequent watering may be necessary until seedlings and cuttings get established. But once they have developed a good root system, water them at regular intervals.
- The roots of most plants hate sitting in water. Like every other plant tissue, roots need to breathe.
- They literally drown if all the air pockets in the soil are filled with water all the time. Even when the top soil looks dry, the lower layers could be soaking wet.
- Frequently watered plants remain tender, and wilt very easily in the sun.
- When the interval between subsequent watering is gradually increased, plants toughen up and learn to be survivors.

However, too much water stress can decrease the yield of some vegetables.

Shallow Watering

- This is another watering mistake committed by those who water their plants with a hand-held garden hose.
- You spray the top growth, washing down the dust on the leaves and giving the entire plant a nice shower.
- Satisfied, you move on unmindful of the fact that the roots have got very little water. When you see the plants looking rather tired in the afternoon sun, you may give them another quick shower.

- Plants drink water through their roots.
- Wilted crowns do recover rapidly when they are sprayed with water, but that is because it helps cut down the transpiration rate.
- Shallow watering results in shallow root run. Plants become dependent on frequent watering.
- They become prone to toppling over and wilting quickly since their roots have not grown deep into the soil to anchor them and to draw water from the reservoirs in the lower layers of soil.
- Cut on the frequency of watering, but water the plants deeply every time. Drip irrigation or a leaky hose watering system ensures deep watering.
- They help save water too.
- Planting Sun Lovers in the Shade
- We all know plants have this unique ability to make food in their leaves with just sunlight, water and air. But sometimes we plant a tomato variety guaranteed to be a prolific bearer close to a tree.
- We may be overjoyed at the luxurious growth, only to be disappointed by the low yield. The poor plant was making a lot of leaves to maximize food production, but it just wasn't enough.
- There are some woodland plants that have evolved to survive in shady spots, but if you plant sun-loving plants there, they just will not thrive.
- Tomatoes and most other veggies do best in

areas where they can get uninterrupted sun throughout the day.

- If you mainly have a shady garden, you cannot hope to grow a lot of vegetables other than some greens. Clear out an area for your vegetable patch.

Planting Out of Season

- It is hard to believe seasons have such a hold on plants.
- Many of us probably have planted seeds or cuttings at the wrong time of the year and watch them put out a bit of growth in the beginning and then quit.
- Seasons are not much of an issue in tropical areas as long as the young plants are given plenty of water.
- But it is quite another story up north.
- Planting out tender seedling too early in spring leaves them at the mercy of late frosts. Delay a bit, and you may miss the chance to get vigorous growth and yield before the rising temperatures play spoilsport.
- Cool season veggies and summer flowers have to be planted at their respective times.
- Beware of end-of-season bargain offers by mail-order companies. By the time the order reaches you, it might be too late to plant them.
- Some seeds are viable for only a short period, so preserving them for the next season may not be a good idea.
- Follow the gardening calendar of your area and listen to the advice of local gardeners for best results.

Not Pruning Bushes and Trees

- Pruning is hard work, but going lax on this seasonal task is one mistake new gardeners make.
- With bushes grown for ornamental purposes, the prized shape and structure are soon lost.
- The yield of fruit trees and berry bushes practically depends on meticulous pruning.
- Left unpruned, the unnecessary branches and suckers zap them of all the energy that should have been directed towards flowering and fruit setting.
- Some fruits grow only on new growth, so unless you prompt the plant to put out new shoots by hard pruning every year, you will be left without much fruit in the next season.
- When you plant an ornamental/fruit tree or shrub, take pains to learn the right pruning technique.
- It is even more important than watering and fertilizing schedules.
- Hard Pruning at the Wrong Time

Have you ever pruned a hydrangea bush real hard in fall because it looked nearly dead?

- You have probably removed all the dormant flower buds that would have bloomed the following year. Some plants bear flowers on old branches while others put out new flowering branches after pruning.
- You should first learn about the flowering pattern of your bush and schedule the pruning accordingly.

- Since pruning instigates new growth in most plants, those that bear flowers and fruits late in the growing season should be pruned once they have gone into dormancy.
- Early pruning will make them put out tender shoots that will suffer frost damage.
- Spring flowering trees and bushes can be pruned immediately after they have finished the show so that they get a long window to develop new growth before the growing season is over.
- Maintain a pruning calendar for the plants in your garden to avoid mistakes.

Using Weed Killers on the Wrong day
- You sprayed the herbicide on a patch of lawn overgrown with weeds, but the next day you find the nearby flower beds decimated.
- There are selective herbicides that kill only the dicot weeds in the lawn and spare the grass. But the spray was carried by the wind to the dicots growing happily in the flower beds too.
- Another mistake is using these chemicals when there's any danger of rains.
- The runoff water will carry them off to wreak damage elsewhere. Chemical herbicides are best avoided, but if you do use them in your garden, choose sunny and windless days.

More importantly, some garden weeds posses extraordinary health benefits. Make sure you know what they are and don't kill these off!

Planting Invasive Plants

- Almost every gardener has fallen in love with a beautiful plant on his/her travels and has brought it home, not realizing they are considered noxious weeds in that area.
- Just because you don't see certain plants in your locality, it doesn't mean they are not invasive.
- Probably years of eradication measures and campaigning or strict rules have managed to keep them out, and you could have just undone all that.
- Whether you gather seeds or plants from the wild or get planting materials from a distant friend or relative, or order them online, check beforehand if they are invasive in your area or not.

Once established, it is hard work, or nearly impossible, to root them out.

Planting Single Self-Sterile Plants

- Have you purchased a berry bush or a young tree and waited for years only to be disappointed when none of the flowers turned into fruit?
- If you have planted a self-sterile variety, you have two options: get rid of it or plant another one and wait for years again.
- Some blueberry plants need two of the same type for successful pollination.
- But it takes two different types of apple trees to give you fruit. Not only that, they should

have the same blooming time.
- Some apple trees produce sterile pollen, so you will need a third tree in the premises. It is a complex matter.
- Some plums and pears are only partially self-sterile, and they manage to grow a few fruit. But they do much better in company.

If you don't want to try your luck, choose your plants with the help of knowledgeable suppliers, or stick to self-fertile varieties.

Scaring Away Pollinators with Pesticides
- Being too handy with pesticides is a big mistake overzealous gardener make.
- We are not talking about contaminating the earth here, although it is a great concern.
- If you find too few vegetables and fruits after meticulously watering and fertilizing your plants and keeping off pests and weeds with frequent spraying, you could have scared off the pollinators.
- It is hard to watch pests chomping away on your well-tended veggies, but remember that all the critters visiting your vegetable patch are not your enemies.
- You need insect pollinators to ensure a good crop.

Planting Trees too Close to the House
- You had zeroed in on the perfect tree for your landscape after extensive research, but now you are contemplating cutting it down.

- You had made the mistake of planting it too close to the house.
- The fully grown tree is literally a threat to your safety, let alone other problems like too much shade, constant dampness and fallen leaves and flowers making a mess around the house.
- It is never a good idea to plant tall trees close to your home. You may think you can keep it under control with regular pruning, but who will control the roots beneath the soil?
- They can spread and swell, making the foundation of the house unstable.

CHAPTER TWO

WHAT ARE FRUITS?

Fruits are the edible fleshy part of a tree or a plant that contains seeds. Fruits come in a variety of flavors, including sweet, sour, bittersweet, and many more. They are great sources of many nutrients required by our body.

TYPES OF FRUITS

There are 8 main types of fruits. They are:

SIMPLE FRUIT

These fruits develop from the ripening of a single ovary of a flower. Simple fruits are of two types, dry and fleshy. Dry simple fruits can be dehiscent or indehiscent. Brazil nuts, strawberries, coconut, walnuts, hazelnuts, etc., are some dry simple fruits. Fleshy simple fruits are those that have a partial or full fleshy pericarp (fruit wall) on maturity. Some examples include cherry, tomato, olives, peach, plums, and cranberry.

AGGREGATE FRUIT

These fruits develop from multiple ovaries of a single flower. There are four main types of aggregate fruits, including follicles, achenes, drupelets, and berries. Raspberry, blackberry, and custard apple are some examples.

MULTIPLE FRUIT

Multiple fruits originate from an inflorescence, which means a cluster of flowers. Each of these flowers individually produces a fruit and the fruits, on maturity, come in the form of a single mass. Pineapple, figs, mulberry, etc., are some multiple fruits.

BERRIES

Berry is a type of simple fruit as it develops from a single ovary of a single flower. Cranberry and blueberry are the two most common examples of berries.

ACCESSORY FRUIT

Any fruit whose edible part comes from the ovary, as well as other parts of the flower, is an accessory fruit. It can be simple, multiple, or an aggregate fruit. Most common examples include pineapple, apple, stone fruit, and strawberry.

SEEDLESS FRUIT

Seedless fruits mature in two ways. The first is where the fruit develops without parthenocarpy, whereas the second is where pollination stimulates fruit development. These are the most valuable fruits as they are consumed by a majority of people.

Growing fruits in your garden doesn't have to be chore. You're only a few steps away from fresh, bountiful fruit plants and we have the tips and tricks to help you get started.

The first step is to choose your plants. You'll find fruit trees, berry bushes, and vines sold three different ways bare root, balled and burlapped, and in a container depending on the time of year and where you shop.

WAYS TO PLANT FRUITS

Bare Root: Bare-root plants are typically available in late winter or early spring and are purchased while they're dormant and leafless. They're usually the least expensive way to purchase plants because they don't have the cost of soil or containers associated with them.

Balled and Burlapped: Balled-and-burlapped fruit trees and shrubs, often simply referred to as b-&-b, are available from spring to fall. They feature a rootball that's wrapped in a sheet of burlap or a similar material. Balled-and-burlapped plants are usually the largest specimens your nursery offers.

Container: Container-grown fruits are most commonly available and easiest to plant. Liked balled-and-burlapped plants, they're available throughout the year and come in a wide range of sizes.

Planting Tips

1. No matter which method you use to plant your fruit trees, berry bushes, or vines, water them well after planting. Spread a 2- to 3-inch-deep layer of mulch over the soil around the plant; this helps the soil maintain moisture longer so you have to water less. It also

     helps to control weed growth.

2. You may need to stake newly planted fruit trees, especially if they are bare-root or if they're in a windy location and want to tip over. Support them only for the first year or two; remove the stakes after that so your trees can develop a sturdy trunk and root system.

3. One of the simplest ways to support a young tree is to use a single stake about as tall as the tree. Drive the stake in the ground about 18 inches deep and about 6 inches away from the edge of the planting hole. Use heavy wire wrapped by a section of old garden hose and tie the tree to the stake using a figure-8 pattern. (The hose prevents the wire from grinding against the bark.)

Test Garden Tip: Avoid pulling the wire tight because it can damage the tree. The trunk should be able to move lightly in any direction if you push against it.

HOW TO PRUNE

No matter what trees, shrubs, or vines you're growing, it's a good idea to prune out any dead or diseased branches and stems. This helps the plant look better and can prevent disease from spreading. Prune out wayward stems that block pathways, driveways, or grow into the side of a house or other structures. Remove branches that cross and rub against one another; as the bark gets rubbed off, it makes the tree more susceptible to disease.

It's best to prune most fruit trees in late fall, winter, or early spring when they're dormant and leafless. Avoid pruning them in early fall—otherwise you make the trees more susceptible to winter injury. Currants and gooseberries also should be pruned in the dormant season, removing approximately one-third of their oldest stems. Grapes and kiwi vines require severe pruning during the dormant season to keep them productive. Most raspberries and blackberries fruit on two-year-old canes. Remove the old canes in summer right after they are done bearing. Tip prune them in summer to make them branch.

Test Garden Tip: Dip your pruning shears in rubbing alcohol or a 10 percent bleach solution between cuts. This prevents the disease from spreading to healthy branches. Dip pruning shears in oil after use to prevent corrosion.

WATERING AND FEEDING YOUR FRUITS

Watering: Most fruits require consistent moisture to produce well. The exact amount to give them depends on soil type, weather conditions, and what kinds of fruits you're growing. For example, you'll need to water plants in sandy soils more often than those in clay. And plants use more water during hot, windy conditions with low humidity than if the weather is cool, humid, and cloudy.

Regardless, apply enough water to moisten the root zone at least 6 inches deep. Soaker hoses and drip irrigation systems are two efficient ways to give your plants the water they need. These methods reduce water use (by applying it just to the root zone there's little lost to evaporation) and help prevent disease by keeping the foliage dry.

Feeding: Not sure if you need to feed your fruits? Start by getting to know your soil and the basics of fertilizer. The best way of evaluating your ground is to have a soil test done. Most university cooperative extension services provide this service for a fee. Some commercial garden centers and professional soil testing laboratories do so as well. You might be tempted to add more fertilizer than the packaging instructions recommend, but resist the urge. Overfertilization can burn plant roots, causing injury to the plant. Fruiting trees and shrubs that get excess fertilizer, especially nitrogen, may flower and produce less than plants that are not overfertilized.

In many regions you may need to acidify the soil to grow blueberries. Adding elemental sulfur to the soil will lower the pH, making the soil more acidic. Use your soil-test results to tell you what your soil's current pH is, then use the instructions on the sulfur bag to determine how much you need to add for your blueberries.

INSECT CONTROL

If you grow fruits, you'll almost certainly find insects attacking them at some point. If a pesticide is necessary, use the least toxic alternative. Insecticidal soap is effective on most soft-bodied pests such as aphids and spider mites. A forceful spray of water from a garden hose may knock down the population of pests, too. Bt (Bacillus thuringiensis) is a natural bacteria that controls the larvae of moths and butterflies, such as those of leafrollers.

A dormant-oil spray is an effective means of controlling many early-season insects such as borers. During the growing season you can use pheromone traps to detect when insects are present and time pesticide controls accordingly.

Apple maggots are small flies that lay eggs in apples. The eggs hatch into worms that tunnel through the fruit. Control the insect by destroying affected fruit before or when it falls on the ground, use red-sticky traps to catch the flies, or by using an insecticide labeled for use on apple maggots in midsummer.

Codling moths feed on apples, creating small holes surrounded by dead tissue. Control this pest by spraying with an insecticide containing Bt in spring, just as the flowers fade. Or try using pheromone traps.

Plum curculio is a mottled brown beetle that causes misshapen fruits that rot and fall off the tree. Lay a sheet under young trees and shake them in late spring or early summer; the beetles will fall off the plant and you can throw them in the trash. Or spray with an insecticide containing neem oil.

Slugs attack fruits such as strawberries. You can control slugs by using a slug bait or spreading horticultural-grade diatomaceous earth over the ground around your plants.

DISEASE CONTROL

Keep diseases to a minimum by providing good air circulation throughout the orchard and garden so that plants dry quickly. Avoid splashing water on the foliage of your fruits. Remove and destroy diseased plants as they develop. Some diseases spread by insects, so keeping the insect population in check helps prevent disease problems. When possible, grow varieties resistant to diseases such as apple scab and cedar-apple rust. Dormant lime sulfur sprays control many fruit fungal diseases.

Black knot often attacks plums, prunes, cherries, and peaches. It looks like black, warty growths on branches that kill them. Control it by selecting resistant varieties, cutting out young branches as soon as the disease starts to manifest, and using a fungicide labeled for use on black knot.

Cedar-apple rust is a disease that causes bright yellow spots on apple leaves and horn-like growths on leaves and young fruits. Use a fungicide labeled for use on cedar-apple rust to help control it.

Fire blight is common on apples and pears, attacking branches, fruits, and flowers. Control it by pruning infected branches out and treating with a bactericide labeled for use for fire blight.

Mildews, including powdery and downy mildew, attack

many fruits. Try to keep foliage dry as much as you can and prune and train the plants to encourage good air circulation. Apply a fungicide labeled for use on mildew when necessary.

Scab often attacks apples after periods of wet, spring weather. It causes scab-like wounds on leaves and fruits. Control it by planting scab-resistant varieties, removing any affected foliage and fruit, or using fungicides labeled for use on scab.

Viruses often cause mottled or misshapen growth. Unfortunately they cannot be treated and affected plants are best destroyed. Purchase plants from a reliable source to ensure they're virus-free when you plant them.

PEST CONTROL

Deer, rabbits, voles, and birds may attack fruits if given the chance. Repellents may keep the animals away, but the surest way to protect your fruiting crop is by exclusion. In the cases of deer and rabbits that means erecting a fence or other enclosure to protect the plants.

Voles chew bark of fruit trees and shrubs over winter. Place a hardware cloth ring around the trunk of fruit trees or around entire shrubs over winter to protect them from voles. Stop birds from stealing or damaging ripe fruit by covering the crop with bird netting.

Preparing the Soil

Good crops need good soil. Most fruit and vegetables like soil that is rich, moist and well-drained, with neutral acidity. There are some exceptions, including blueberries which need acidic soil.

These are best grown in containers filled with ericaceous (acidic) compost. But for the majority of crops, you simply need balanced, good quality soil.

Soil improvers

Digging in plenty of organic matter will improve the structure of your soil and add nutrients for the plants. Some veg growers add well-rotted manure in the autumn ask a local farmer to deliver some for you.

Most veg gardeners simply add compost or leaf mould. These are common soil improvers available from garden centres though you should start making your own compost if you don't already! It's so easy and keeps a constant (and free) supply of extra nutrients to boost your plants.

You can dig some compost or leaf mould into the top few inches of the soil a couple of weeks before planting most vegetables. Or scatter some general-purpose compost over the surface and rake it in.

You can also apply the organic matter over the surface of the soil around established plants as a mulch. This allows the nutrients to feed down into the soil, as well as helping to retain moisture and stop weeds growing.

BEST FRUIT PLANTS TO GROW IN YOUR GARDEN

There are many fruits you can grow in your home garden, even if you have limited space. But before you plant, put some thought into which fruits grow best in your climate, as well as the placement of your garden. Fruit trees and shrubs can live for many years and require proper sunlight, soil, and air circulation. Here are nine of the best types of fruit to grow in your garden.

Tip

Even if your fruit variety is hardy, frigid and drying winds can kill the tender buds, resulting in no fruit for the season. The same can happen when a late spring frost hits the buds. You can't control the weather, but planting in a sheltered location, such as near a fence or hedge, will help.

BLUEBERRIES

Berries are an easy way to try your hand at growing fruit. Blueberries are attractive three-season shrubs with pretty white spring flowers, summer fruit, and gorgeous red fall foliage. Growing blueberries requires some advance work to ensure the soil is acidic enough, but the shrubs should live and produce fruit for years. For a large harvest, you will need two varieties for good pollination.

In cold winter climates, grow highbush blueberries, such as 'Bluecrop'. Gardeners in mild climates should opt for either rabbiteye or southern highbush varieties. You can also grow blueberries in containers. Just be sure to cover your plants with netting to protect them from birds once the fruit arrives.

- USDA Growing Zones: 5 to 7 ('Bluecrop')
- Sun Exposure: Full sun to part shade
- Soil Needs: Rich, acidic, medium to wet moisture, well-draining

STRAWBERRIES

Freshly picked strawberries are well worth the minimal effort it takes to grow them. You have a choice among three types: June bearing, which sets one large crop in June (nice for preserves and freezing); everbearing, which produces two to three smaller harvests per season; and day neutral, which continually sets small amounts of strawberries throughout the season.

Strawberry plants like to spread via runners. But for the best fruit production, limit the runners to just a few plants and prune the rest. Also, pinch off the blossoms in a plant's first season to prevent it from fruiting. This will allow it to put its energy toward developing a healthy root system, which will significantly increase its output the next season. Finally, expect to replace or rejuvenate your strawberry plant every three to five years.

- USDA Growing Zones: 5 to 8 (Fragaria x ananassa)
- Sun Exposure: Full sun
- Soil Needs: Rich, slightly acidic, medium moisture, well-draining

RASPBERRIES AND BLACKBERRIES

Raspberries and blackberries have always been backyard favorites. But older varieties can be rambunctious plants, spreading widely and being covered in thorns that made harvesting a painful chore. Newer cultivars are much better behaved and thornless. Moreover, planting a mix of early, mid-season, and late-season varieties will extend your harvest for weeks.

The plants do require annual pruning to keep them productive, but it is a quick job. The goal with pruning is to thin the plants enough that light and air can reach all parts. This benefits growth and helps to prevent disease.

- USDA Growing Zones: 5 to 8 (Rubus fruticosus)
- Sun Exposure: Full sun to part shade
- Soil Needs: Rich, slightly acidic, moist, well-draining

GRAPES

Although grapevines are not hard to grow, you will face stiff competition at harvest time from birds and other animals. Plus, grapes need some type of trellis or support to grow on. There are also a lot of recommendations on how to prune them, but many people grow them quite successfully with a relaxed approached to pruning.

Check with your local extension office to learn about the best grape varieties for your area. And be sure to note whether a variety is best for eating or winemaking. Most grape varieties need a sunny location with rich soil that has good drainage and air circulation to prevent disease.

- USDA Growing Zones: 5 to 8 (Vitis labrusca 'Concord')
- Sun Exposure: Full sun
- Soil Needs: Rich, medium moisture, well-draining

APPLES

Many gardeners want to grow apples, but they are difficult to grow well because apple trees are prone to many insect and disease problems. Although new cultivars were bred to be hardy, they still require some spraying, covering, or other protection methods. Apple trees also need a great deal of pruning. When pruning, focus on thinning branches to increase the amount of sunlight and airflow that can hit all parts of the tree. This promotes healthy growth and helps to prevent disease.

You'll need two different apple tree varieties for pollination. To save space, you can select trees with multiple varieties grafted onto one trunk, or opt for a small columnar tree that can be grown in a container. Plus, for easier care or if you have limited space, consider the dwarf varieties.

- USDA Growing Zones: 4 to 9 (Malus pumila 'Honeycrisp')
- Sun Exposure: Full sun
- Soil Needs: Rich, medium moisture, well-draining

CHERRIES

Cherries are one of the easiest fruit trees to grow and care for. They require minimal to no pruning and are rarely plagued by pests or diseases. Sweet cherries need two trees for cross-pollination unless you plant a tree with two different varieties grafted on it. Moreover, you can get away with just one tree if you are growing sour baking cherries.

Prune your cherry tree in the winter while it is still dormant, and fertilize it in the early spring. Moreover, these trees aren't very drought tolerant. So ensure that they get watering or rainfall at least weekly or more during hot weather.

- USDA Growing Zones: 5 to 8 (Prunus avium 'Bing')
- Sun Exposure: Full sun
- Soil Needs: Rich, moist, well-draining

PEACHES

Peach trees tend to be small enough to fit in most backyard sizes. And when the peaches are ripening, you can smell their sweetness several yards away. Plus, a benefit to growing this thin-skinned fruit yourself is you'll get to enjoy the freshest produce straight from the tree, rather than the old and potentially bruised options at the supermarket.

These trees do require some pruning to keep the branches productive and at a manageable height. Thinning young trees helps them to produce smaller crops of large peaches, rather than heavy crops of tiny peaches. Peach trees are typically pruned into an open V with three to five main branches that allow light and air to hit the center.

- USDA Growing Zones: 5 to 9 (Prunus persica)
- Sun Exposure: Full sun
- Soil Needs: Rich, loamy, medium moisture, well-draining

FIGS

Fig trees are surprisingly easy to grow either in the ground or in containers. They do not require much pruning and are usually pest free. Most fig varieties are only reliably hardy down to USDA hardiness zone 7, but there are a few new cultivars that are hardier.

If you choose to grow your fig tree in a container and move it indoors for the winter, keep the container small. The more confined the roots are, the smaller the top of the tree will remain. It will be much easier to move, and you will still get plenty of figs.

- USDA Growing Zones: 6 to 9 (Ficus carica)
- Sun Exposure: Full sun to part shade
- Soil Needs: Rich, moist, well-draining

MELONS

If you aren't ready for the commitment of a tree or shrub, you can still grow delicious melons in your garden or in containers. Melons need a lot of sun and heat. They also require ample space, as they grow on vines that can easily reach 20 feet or more. It is possible to grow melons on a trellis, but you will need to choose a variety with small fruits. Large melons, such as watermelon, can become so heavy that they will drop right off the plant.

Plant your melons after the danger of frost has passed for the season. Water regularly as they grow and become established. Then, once the fruits start to appear, you can back off a bit on watering.

- USDA Growing Zones: 2 to 11 annual (Citrullus lanatus)
- Sun Exposure: Full sun
- Soil Needs: Rich, loamy, moist, well-draining

COCNCLUSION

Watching a seed blossom under your care to become food on your and your family's plates is gratifying. Growing your own food is one of the most purposeful and import- ant things a human can do it's work that directly helps you thrive, nourish your family and maintain your health. Caring for your plants and waiting as they blossom and "fruit" before your eyes is an amazing sense of accomplish- ment.

With recalls on peanut butter, spinach, tomatoes and more, many people are concerned about food safety in our global food marketplace. When you responsibly grow your own food, you don't have to worry about contamination that may occur at the farm, manufacturing plant or transportation process. This means that when the whole world is avoiding tomatoes, for example, you don't have to go without you can trust that your food is safe and healthy to eat.

Americans throw away about $600 worth of food each year! It's a lot easier to toss a moldy orange that you paid $0.50 for than a perfect red pepper that you patiently watched ripen over the course of several weeks. When it's "yours," you will be less likely to take it for granted and more likely to eat it (or preserve it) before it goes to waste.

Even if you don't have a big backyard or any yard for

that matter you can still grow food. Consider container gardening if you have a sunny balcony or patio or an indoor herb garden on a windowsill. You'll be amazed at how many tomatoes or peppers can grow out of one pot.

Whatever your motivation for breaking ground on your own backyard garden, chances are good that you'll take pleasure in this new healthy hobby, and that your wallet, the environment, your body and your taste buds will thank you.